A special thanks
to everyone
who has helped make
Know Yourself
what it is today.

Dear Reader

Knowing yourself is truly the beginning of all wisdom. We give young learners the building blocks they need to start their unique journey of self-discovery: an understanding of human anatomy — literally how we are put together. Knowledge of one's own human body is an empowering context on which anyone can build.

Learning about the body and mind at a young age sets the foundation for honoring one's physical form, develops confidence, and begins the discovery of who we are meant to be.
Now that's real power.

The Know Yourself Team

Quick-Start Guide

Hello Know Yourselfers!

Follow these steps to start a new journey and explore the circulatory system. Have fun on this quest and remember - A mind in motion is never stagnant!

1

Grab an atlas or a sketch you draw while going to China

Locate China on your atlas, or find an online map of the world.

2

Read THIS Story: Adventure 3

Pinky and Sketch come face-to-face with the warrior monk Tianyuan and the Shaolin. Will the Time Skaters get past the pirate threat?

3

Get equipped!

Gather your supplies and prepare for your activities. In the harmony of the system you will find the whole.

Table of Contents

QUICK-START GUIDE III

Hello Adventurer! 1

TIME SKATERS ADVENTURE 3 3

LEARNING CALENDAR 22

Home Inventory Checklist 24

PART 1 • KNOW YOUR HISTORY 26

LEARN: Ancient China 26
ACTIVITIES: • Silk Road Secrets 30
• Imperial Examinations 33
• Go Play Go 34
• Know Your Script 36
• Fancy Fans 38
• Learning with Animals 40
• Ancient China Crossword 42
• Know Your History Information Review 44

PART 2 • KNOW YOUR CIRCULATORY SYSTEM   46

LEARN: Flow Through Circulation:
The Heart of the Matter 50

Blood on the Move 52

Know Your Calm 60

ACTIVITIES: • Feel the Beat:
Taking a Trip Through Your Body 62

• Heartbeat Hopscotch 64

• Pour Your Heart Out 68

• Know Your Flow 72

• Go with the Flow 74

• Breath of Fresh Air 78

• Circulatory System Word Search 80

• Know Your Circulatory System
Information Review 82

PART 3 • KNOW YOUR APPETITE 84

RECIPES: • Easy Chinese Moon Cakes 86

• Chinese Dumplings 89

Thoughts for Young Chefs 92

PART 4 • CUMULATIVE INFORMATION REVIEW   94

Further Reading 99

Hello Adventurer!

Welcome to Adventure 3 - The Circulatory System.

In this workbook, you will learn about Ancient China and your body's circulatory system. There will be information to read, activities to complete, and quizzes to take when you are ready to challenge yourself! Take your time along the way - spend
as much or as little time as you like on each activity, and do not forget to use additional resources to learn more about the topics you are interested in.

Good luck, and have fun!

Destination: Ancient China!

THE TIME TRAVEL CLOCK READS 1553

Get ready to start flowing!

LEARN ABOUT
The Circulatory System
This bodily highway delivers all the nutrients you need!

VISIT
Ancient China
As pirates threaten the coast, the civilians must unify if they are to withstand the assault.

MEET
Tianyuan and the Shaolin Monks
as they harness their internal strength.

(Huānyíng)*
That means "Welcome!" in Mandarin Chinese.

***Say it like this:** "hoo-ahn-**YING**"
The strongest syllable is shown in CAPITALS.

Enter this portal for....

Time Skaters Adventure 3
The Zen is Mightier
than the Sword

THE CIRCULATORY SYSTEM

THE CIRCULATORY SYSTEM

THE CIRCULATORY SYSTEM

RAD.

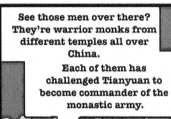

See those men over there? They're warrior monks from different temples all over China.

Each of them has challenged Tianyuan to become commander of the monastic army.

Legend says the other monks used magic to make their abilities extra powerful.

YOU SAY THAT YOU'RE STRONG ENOUGH TO FIGHT OFF THE PIRATE THREAT, YET DON'T CARRY SO MUCH AS A STICK.

YOU ARE PATHETIC AND SMALL--HOW CAN YOU EXPECT TO FIGHT AN ARMY WITHOUT A SWORD?

HEH.

YOU ARE SMALL-MINDED, BROTHER XIANG.

THOUGH YOU MAY REQUIRE A WEAPON TO FIGHT, ALL THE STRENGTH I NEED RESIDES WITHIN MY HEART.

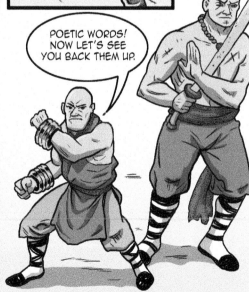

POETIC WORDS! NOW LET'S SEE YOU BACK THEM UP.

THE CIRCULATORY SYSTEM

THE CIRCULATORY SYSTEM

THE CIRCULATORY SYSTEM

THE CIRCULATORY SYSTEM

THE CIRCULATORY SYSTEM

THE CIRCULATORY SYSTEM

I THINK I UNDERSTAND.

WHAT I WAS LOOKING FOR BEFORE...

WAS HERE THE ENTIRE TIME!

THE SKULL-STYLE MASTER CAME BY WAY OF THIS HILLTOP.

I CAN ONLY HOPE THAT THIS ODD SYMBOL CAN HELP RETURN YOU TO HIS TRAIL.

IT'S ALMOST DINNERTIME. I'LL SEE YOU TWO IN THE DINING HALL.

HANK? ARE YOU SEEING THIS?

FZZZZ

THE CIRCULATORY SYSTEM

Learning Calendar

Part 1

Know Your History

Estimated hours
4 hours of fun

Locate China on a world map using a globe, atlas, or an online map (like this one: https://knowyourself.com/maps)

Read the comic *Time Skaters Adventure 3 - The Zen is Mightier than the Sword*. Find it at the beginning of this Adventure Guide!

Gather the adventure equipment you'll need from around the house - find the checklist on pages 24 and 25!

Meditate on the past with *Know Your History*.

Dip into *Know Your Script*.

Discover *Silk Road Secrets*.

Get moving and *Go Play Go*.

Fabricate *Fancy Fans*.

Solve *Ancient China Crossword*.

Take *Know Your History Information Review*.

Part 2

Know Your Circulatory System

Keep current and *Know Your Circulatory System*.

De-stress with *Know Your Calm*.

Hop to *Heartbeat Hopscotch*.

Complete *Pour Your Heart Out*.

Go *with the Flow.*

Complete the *Circulatory System Word Search.*

Take *Know Your Circulatory System Information Review.*

Part **3**

Know Your Appetite

Get Inspired inspiration in *Know Your Appetite.*

Read the recipes on the following pages. Make a shopping list, purchase ingredients, and get your kitchen ready!

Make *Easy Chinese Moon Cakes* and *Chinese Dumplings.*

Share your dishes with your family. Discuss *Thoughts for Young Chefs* around the table!

Part **4**

Show What You Know!

Take the Adventure 3 *Cumulative Information Review.*

Check out *Further Reading* for more opportunities to learn.

Great job on all your hard work!

Home Inventory Checklist

Ask your parents to help you find these items around the house. These are some of the tools you will need on your adventure. Don't worry if you can't find every single one - you'll be able to use your imagination.

- [ ] **Markers, colored pencils, and/or crayons**
  - Know Your Script, Silk Road Secrets, Go Play Go, Fancy Fans

- [ ] **Large piece of blank paper**
  - Go Play Go

- [ ] **80 colored beads, stones, or other objects to be used as game pieces** (40 for each side)
  - Go Play Go

- [ ] **Construction paper or other paper**
  - Fancy Fans

- [ ] **Tape**
  - Fancy Fans, Pour Your Heart Out

- [ ] **Sidewalk chalk**
  - Heartbeat Hopscotch

- [ ] **Toothpick or scissors**
  - Pour Your Heart Out

- [ ] **Large pan** (or a sink)
  - Pour Your Heart Out

- [ ] **Wide-mouthed jar**
  - Pour Your Heart Out

- [ ] **Water**
  - Pour Your Heart Out, Know Your Flow

- [ ] **2 straws (one red, one blue)**
  - Pour Your Heart Out

☐ Balloon
   - Pour Your Heart Out

☐ A soft blanket or a yoga mat
   - Go with the Flow

☐ Clear tupperware or jar
   - Know Your Flow

☐ Red food coloring
   - Know Your Flow

☐ O-shaped cereal
   - Know Your Flow

☐ 1 plastic sealed bag
   - Know Your Flow

☐ White beans
   - Know Your Flow

☐ Lentils
   - Know Your Flow

☐ Stopwatch
   - Feel the Beat

Be creative if you don't have something on the list.

✓ Check the items off when you've found them!

Ancient China

While famous for their kung fu, the Shaolin monks didn't always practice this martial art.

Kung fu was introduced by Da Mo, a monk from India also known as Bodhidharma. Da Mo had given up his life as a prince to become a monk. In the year 527, he visited the Shaolin Temple spreading the teachings of Buddhism.

coloring
opportunity

Upon arriving at the Shaolin Temple, Da Mo decided to stay in a cave in one of the mountains behind the monastery. There, he meditated for nine years. Da Mo believed in discipline and dedication through meditation.

He taught that looking into yourself would allow you to see your true nature, a notion that would later become known as "Zen." During his meditation, Da Mo developed a series of movements and breathing that eventually became kung fu, which means "learned skill."

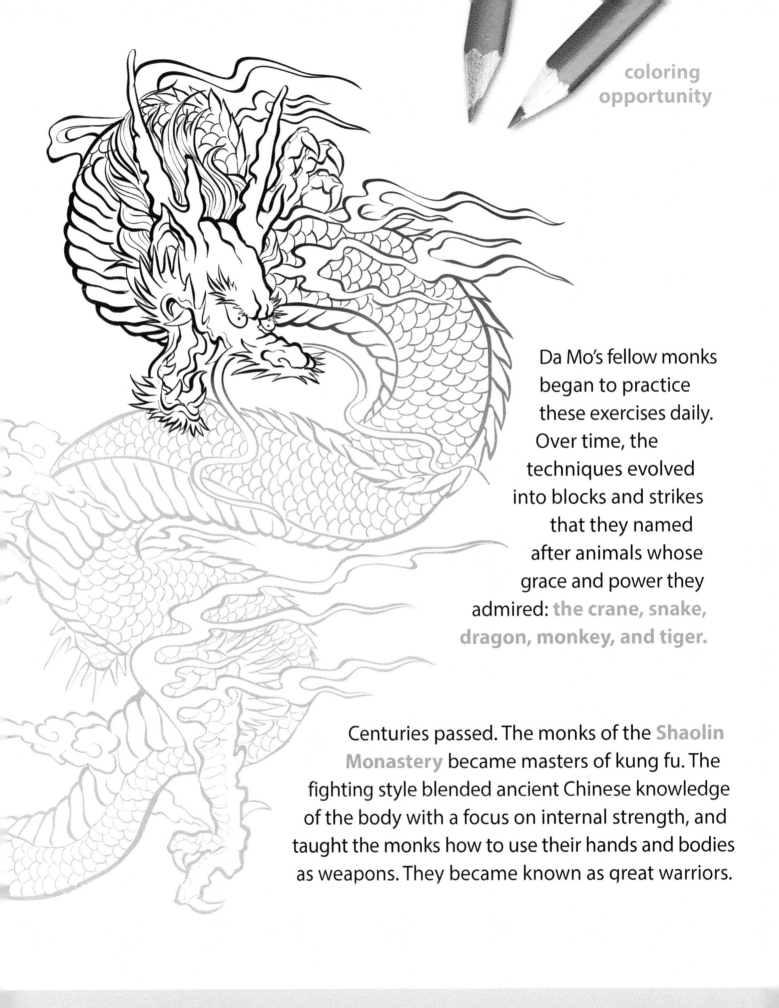

coloring opportunity

Da Mo's fellow monks began to practice these exercises daily. Over time, the techniques evolved into blocks and strikes that they named after animals whose grace and power they admired: **the crane, snake, dragon, monkey, and tiger.**

Centuries passed. The monks of the Shaolin Monastery became masters of kung fu. The fighting style blended ancient Chinese knowledge of the body with a focus on internal strength, and taught the monks how to use their hands and bodies as weapons. They became known as great warriors.

Tianyuan was a Chinese monk who was one of the Shaolin leaders. In 1553, when pirates attacked Chinese merchant ships, the government asked Tianyuan and his followers to help defend the country. Eight other monks decided to challenge Tianyuan with swords to prevent him from taking charge. Tianyuan famously defeated all the men at once (using only an iron bar from a nearby gate). He won the right to lead the Shaolin alongside the Chinese army. Together, they fought the pirates and protected both the merchants and their coastal towns.

Kung fu was also in harmony with the monks' faith. Buddhism called for compassion, justice, and honesty, as well as physical and spiritual fitness. Ultimately, the monks did kung fu not for combat, but for personal cultivation:

To know themselves!

Can you imagine traveling on camelback along an enormous trade route from China to Europe? This would take quite a long time!

The Silk Road was established in a time of growing success and wealth in the Chinese and Roman empires. The people living within each empire began to thrive, and as a result, so did their desire for luxury goods.

One luxurious good was silk. No one from outside of China knew how silk was made for three thousand years! The secrecy surrounding silk production made the material very valuable to people in the rest of the world. Greek and Roman traders would pay gold and silver in exchange for the mysterious material!

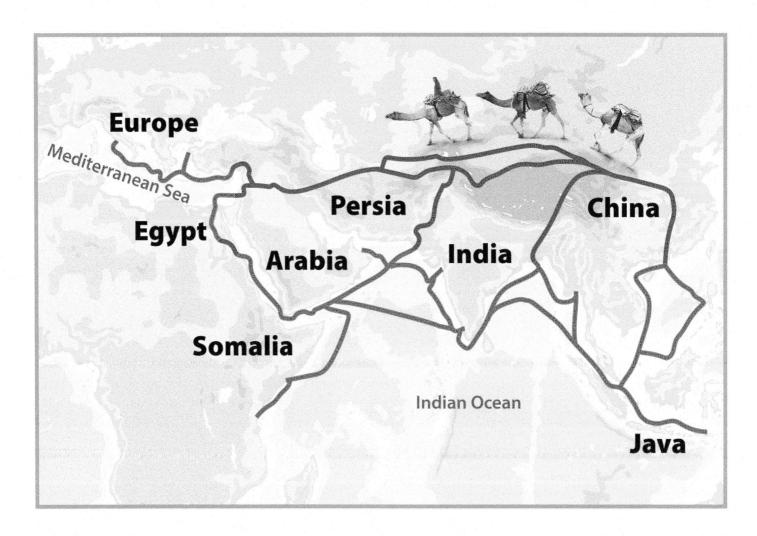

Silk surprisingly comes from a bug called the silkworm. These little invertebrates are able to spin thousands of feet of silk around themselves to form cocoons. Inside of their cocoons, they rest and slowly transform to become moths.

Another good that the Ancient Chinese traded was paper. Paper was originally made from tree bark and hemp, and was used to package other items.

Can you color in the silkworm, cocoon, and moth below?

Materials:

- **Markers, colored pencils, and/or crayons**

Directions:

1. Bring the silkworm's story to life! Draw in the silkworm, cocoon, and moth using your markers, colored pencils, and/or crayons.

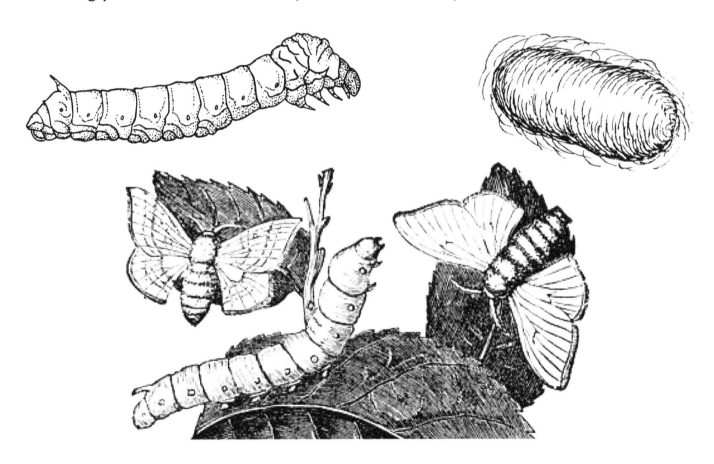

Silk Road Secrets

Can you think of anything you have exchanged, or 'traded', this week? Write down your experience trading.

_____

_____

_____

_____

_____

_____

_____

_____

_____

_____

_____

During the Song Dynasty, the Chinese government began to rely on a new system to recruit people called the Imperial Examinations. Instead of allowing people to gain positions of power based on their social status alone, they created a series of tests to determine who was eligible for government jobs. While the wealthy were able to hire tutors and had more time to study, anyone could try to pass the exams and get a good job for themselves. Emperor Taizong of Song implemented a rule that nobody could know whose exam they were grading. Examiners couldn't even hold exams in their home town, to try and make it as fair as possible.

Imagine that you needed to choose people to be part of your court and help you go about your day.

What would you test them on? Mathematics? Artistic skill? Ability to bake cookies?

_____

_____

_____

_____

_____

Go Play Go

Weiqi, or Go, is a game so ancient, we aren't even entirely sure when it was invented. The earliest written records of the game are from 548 B.C.! And it wasn't just a game -- ancient Chinese aristocrats considered it one of the four essential skilled arts of a scholar, along with playing the guqin (a stringed instrument), calligraphy, and painting. From China, it spread to Korea and Japan in the 5th Century, and now it is played all over the world. In fact, in 1996, the first game of Go was played in Outer Space!

Easy to learn but difficult to master, Go is traditionally played on a 19-by-19 board. Learning on a 9-by-9 board is common, though, and you can make one yourself to practice!

Go is played by placing pieces on the intersections, so you need to make a board with 9 lines side-to-side and 9 lines top to bottom, or 8 boxes in each direction, as pictured on the next page.

Materials:

- **Large piece of paper**
- **Pen**
- **40 pieces for each player** (stones, colored beads, pieces of paper, etc)

Directions:

1. Make your board by making 9 lines horizontally and 9 lines vertically.

2. Take turns by placing your piece on one of the intersections of lines on your board.
   a. You can't do the same thing twice in a row, so if a piece gets removed you can't go right back!

3. If a piece or group of pieces doesn't have an open point adjacent to it, remove it!

4. When both players pass a turn or can't play a piece, add up how many pieces each player has on the board plus how many empty spaces they have surrounded. Whoever has the most wins!

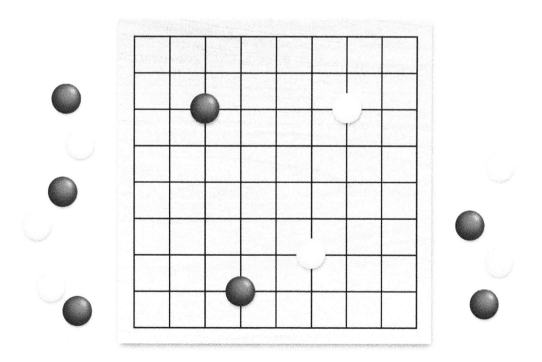

Chinese Calligraphy

Calligraphy is an art form of stylized handwriting. Although it is celebrated in many parts of the world, Chinese calligraphy has evolved its own unique style. This branch of calligraphy focuses on motion and has gained popularity in countries like Taiwan, Japan, Korea, and Vietnam.

Chinese calligraphy focuses on careful use of pressure, speed, and direction of the ink brush to produce thinner or bolder lines. This focus has a calming effect on the mind and body, and results in beautiful art like the characters shown here.

The calligrapher holds the ink brush vertically between their thumb and middle finger. The index finger keeps the brush steady as the calligrapher works.

Materials:

- **Felt-tip pen**
- **Paper**

Directions

Use the chart on the next page as a guide for writing numbers in Chinese calligraphy. We wrote 1553, the year Pinky and Sketch travel to in Adventure 3, to show how smaller numbers combine to make bigger numbers. When you get the hang of these symbols, try writing out today's date (month, day, and year).

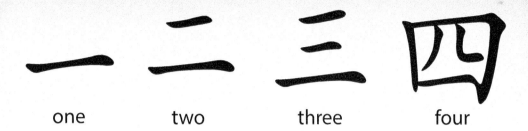

一	二	三	四
one	two	three	four

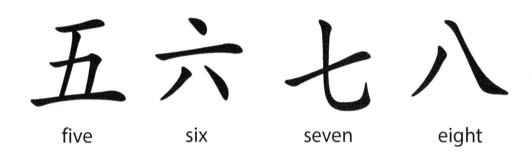

五	六	七	八
five	six	seven	eight

九	十	百	千
nine	ten	hundred	thousand

一 千 五 百 五 十 三

一千 + 五百 + 五十 + 三 = **1553**

1 thousand   5 hundred   5 10's   3

Fancy Fans

The history of Chinese fans goes back thousands of years — archaeologists have even discovered intact fans from the 2nd century B.C. A fan works by creating airflow, which increases the rate at which your sweat evaporates. This helps to cool you off faster. Before air conditioning or electric fans, a fan was effective and easy to carry around, which is probably why this Chinese innovation spread around the world.

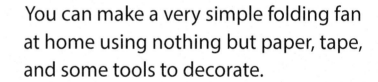

Fans were often decorated with art and poetry, and made out of materials ranging from paper to feathers and bamboo. Folding fans are also used in some performances of Kung Fu!

You can make a very simple folding fan at home using nothing but paper, tape, and some tools to decorate.

Materials:

- **Construction paper or other crafting paper (2 sheets)**

- **Pens and/or markers**

- **Tape**

- **Optional: Feathers, sequins, glitter glue, stickers, etc.**

Directions:

1. Lay your paper down with the short sides touching. Pull one piece over the other about half an inch so they slightly overlap.

2. Use your art skills to make a design, draw a picture or write a message.

3. Starting from one end, fold the paper half an inch over one way and then the other in an accordian fashion. Do this with both pieces of paper.

4. Connect the two pieces of paper by taping the last and first fold together. Do your best to maintain your picture.

5. Hold the accordion shape together so it is very small, and then tape together the bottom inch of the paper to make a grip. Make sure the rest of the fan is still able to spread out!

Now you have a fan you can use to cool yourself off just like people have done across the world for millennia.

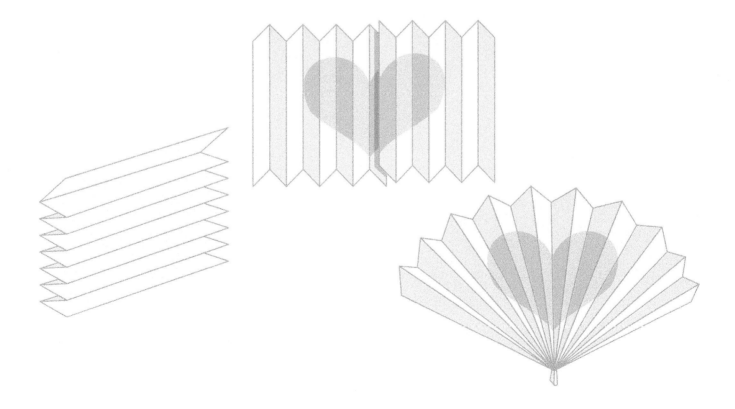

Learning with Animals

When monks developed strikes for Kung Fu, they drew inspiration from the movements of animals. People have been doing this all around the world for years, both for martial arts and for scientific knowledge.

If you have pets at home, try following them around to see how they move, keep their balance, and navigate. You can also watch online videos of more exotic animals and see if there is anything you can pick up.

You might not need to pounce for treats, but one of the best ways to know yourself is to figure out how other living things navigate the world.
Once you've made your fan, see how you can use it to improve your balance, like a bird spreading a wing!

crane

coloring
opportunity

Here are some other animals that the monks admired
for their grace and power.

tiger

dragon

monkey

snake

Ancient China Crossword

After you finish,
check the answer key on page 110.

Across:

3. The _____ monastery was the monastery where monks trained in the martial art of kung fu.

5. A Chinese innovation that helps you cool off by speeding up the evaporation of sweat.

6. A martial art style based on the ancient Chinese knowledge of the body.

8. Another name for Chinese dumplings, a popular and delicious food.

9. A luxurious trade good that originated in Ancient China.

Down:

1. This monk famously defeated eight men at one time (using only an iron bar from a nearby gate).

2. The fourth largest country in the world.

4. Means 'Welcome' in the Mandarin Chinese language.

7. A Chinese cake that is traditionally eaten during the Mid-Autumn festival.

8. An ancient Chinese game, considered to be one of the four essential arts of a scholar by Ancient Chinese aristocrats.

Good work, Adventurers!

Now that you have read some things about Ancient China, let's review what you have learned!

Try to fill in the blanks.

Shaolin monks did not always practice Kung Fu; this practice was introduced by

__ __ __ __ , a monk from __ __ __ __ __ . In the year 527, he visited a Shaolin

Temple to spread the teachings of __ __ __ __ __ __ __ __ .

Kung Fu means __ __ __ __ __ __ __ __ __ __ __ __ and was originally a series

of __ __ __ __ __ __ __ __ __ and __ __ __ __ __ __ __ __ __ .

The blocks and strikes that evolved and which

the martial art is known for were named after

the __ __ __ __ __ __ __ that inspired them.

You can check your answers using the key on page 111.

__ __ __ __ __ __ __ was a famous Chinese monk asked to help defend the

country from __ __ __ __ __ __ __ . Using an iron bar, he defeated __ __ __ __

monks with swords to earn the right to lead.

Despite its martial utility, Kung Fu was primarily studied to aid the monks in their

quest to __ __ __ __ __ __ __ __ __ __ __ __ __ __ __ .

coloring opportunity

Know Your Circulatory System

The Roads Most Traveled

Did you know there is an entire community living inside your body? Like the order of Shaolin monks, tiny cells in your body also work together, doing jobs to keep you healthy.

The Shaolin have a Temple, a central place where lots of things happen, and your body also has a center — **your heart!**
This important organ sends out the blood you need to different areas of your body. In the city of Dengfeng, monks rejuvenate themselves at the Temple with knowledge and training, then use roads to travel out into the world. Your circulatory system uses the heart and blood vessels to do the same thing.

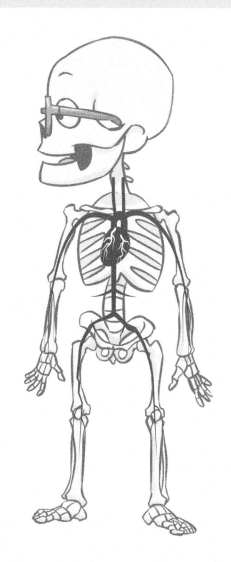

When vehicles travel on city streets, they usually deliver things people need, like food or supplies. Blood carries something you really need: **oxygen**, which you breathe in every few seconds to stay alive. So, when blood travels around your body, it is also making important deliveries.

Sometimes a road only goes one way. That means all the cars travel in the same direction. Your body also has one-way streets that carry blood to and from the heart.

Arteries* are one-way paths that carry blood away from the heart and get smaller and smaller the farther away they get.

Veins* are tunnels going in the opposite direction. They carry blood to the heart from different places in the body.

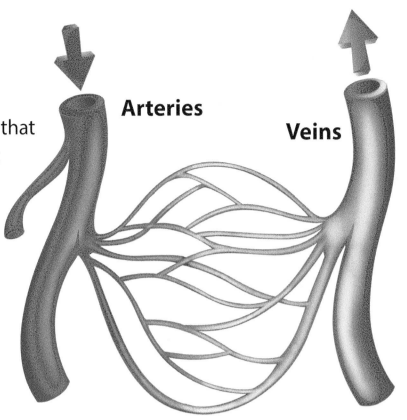

Just like on a roadmap, arteries and veins are spread throughout your body, so blood and oxygen can go everywhere, from the tips of your toes to the top of your head.

In your veins and arteries are tiny doors called valves. These valves help direct the blood down the right path.

*Say them like this:

arteries - "**ARE**-ter-eez"
veins - "**VAY**-nz"

The strongest syllable is always shown in **CAPITALS** and **red**.

Know Your Circulatory System

Your heart has four different areas called **chambers**, which work together to direct your blood flow.

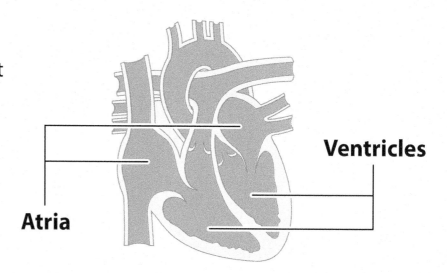

Ventricles

Atria

Atria* are the two chambers at the top of the heart, and they are divided into a left and right side. They receive the blood coming in from the veins, and then release it into the heart's bottom two chambers.

Ventricles* are the two chambers at the bottom of the heart, also divided into left and right. Once they receive the blood from the atria, they send it right back out into the body through the arteries.

Always learning and training, the Shaolin monks work constantly – and so does your busy circulatory system. It is always in motion, pumping the needed blood around the city inside you.

> *Say them like this:
>
> **atria** - "A-tree-uh"
> **ventricles** - "VEN-trih-kuls"
>
> The strongest syllable is always shown in **CAPITALS** and **red**.

How big is your heart?

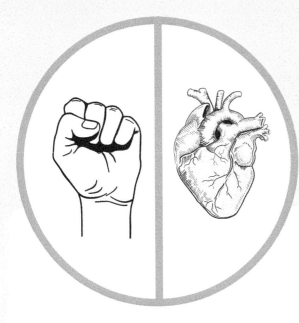

Make a fist with your hand, like you're going do a kung fu punch. That is about the size of your heart.

Although not very big, it is strong.

Draw a heart with the size of your fist.

THE CIRCULATORY SYSTEM

Flow Through Circulation:
The Heart of the Matter

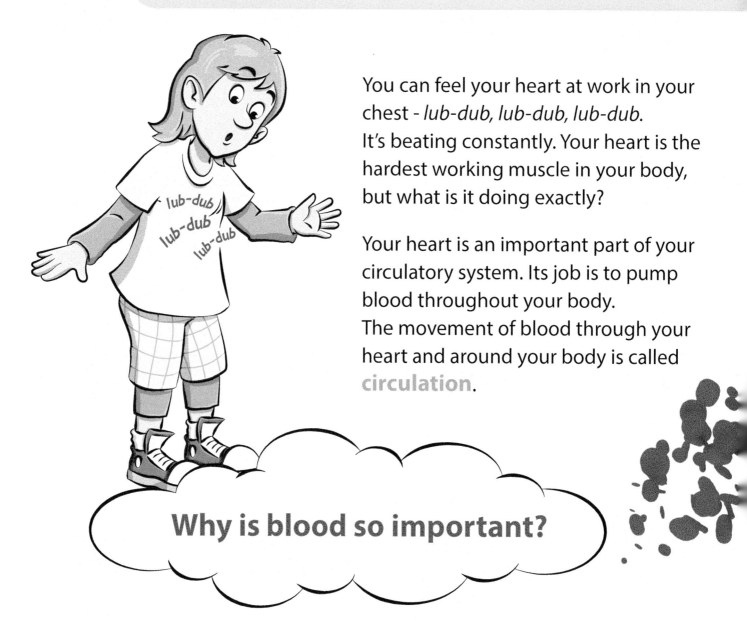

You can feel your heart at work in your chest - *lub-dub, lub-dub, lub-dub.* It's beating constantly. Your heart is the hardest working muscle in your body, but what is it doing exactly?

Your heart is an important part of your circulatory system. Its job is to pump blood throughout your body. The movement of blood through your heart and around your body is called **circulation**.

Why is blood so important?

Blood is responsible for providing your body with oxygen and special chemicals like hormones, as well as for removing waste and carbon dioxide. Your blood contains plasma and three types of blood cells: red blood cells, white blood cells, and platelets. You can learn more about each part on the next page.

White Blood Cells

are part of the immune system. They help your body fight infection from bacteria, viruses, and fungi.

Plasma

is the yellow, watery part of your blood. It carries cells, nutrients, salts, and proteins. It is more than 90% water.

Blood

Red Blood Cells

have hemoglobin, a protein that carries oxygen from your lungs to other parts of your body.

Platelets

are tiny blood cells involved in clotting. If you get scratched, platelets migrate to the cut, clot the blood, and stop the bleeding.

THE CIRCULATORY SYSTEM

Blood on the Move

Look closely at the diagram below. Wow! Is that a road map beneath the skin? The "roads" are really blood vessels. Blood vessels are tubes moving blood to and from your body parts. These vessels work together with your heart to deliver blood where it is needed. There are two types of blood vessels; arteries and veins. Your heart and your blood vessels form the circulatory system, also called the cardiovascular system.

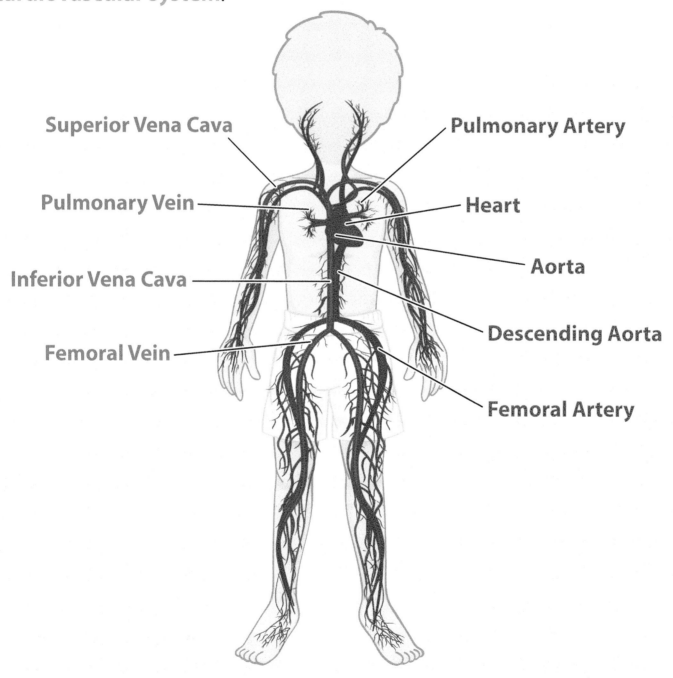

Superior Vena Cava

Pulmonary Artery

Pulmonary Vein

Heart

Inferior Vena Cava

Aorta

Femoral Vein

Descending Aorta

Femoral Artery

Arteries and arterioles (small branches of arteries) are blood vessels that carry blood away from the heart.

To help you remember, think

artery = A = away!

Your body's main artery is the **aorta**.* Can you find it on the diagram? The aorta is the first artery just off the heart. The **aorta and other arteries** are colored red on this diagram. Blood vessels with a red color are carrying blood with oxygen. We call this oxygenated blood.

Veins and venules (very small veins) are colored blue on this diagram. They carry deoxygenated blood to the heart. Deoxygenated means without oxygen.

Our body has a few surprises! There are exceptions to the rule of veins carrying deoxygenated blood and arteries carrying oxygenated blood. You'll see that the pulmonary artery and the pulmonary vein behave the opposite of what is expected.

*Say it like this:

aorta - "a-OR-tuh"

The strongest syllable is always shown in **CAPITALS** and **red**.

When your blood pressure is taken, a nurse or doctor measures the strength of your blood pushing against the sides of your blood vessels.

Blood on the Move

You know that your heart acts like a pump for your blood. It also has other duties. The right side of your heart receives blood from the body and pumps it to the lungs. The left side of the heart does the opposite. It receives blood from the lungs and pumps it out to the body. Check out the steps here!

Follow the path!

Step 1. Deoxygenated blood comes into the **right atrium** of your heart from large veins called the superior vena cava and the inferior vena cava.

Step 2. As the right atrium contracts, it pumps blood into the **right ventricle**, which then pumps it into the **pulmonary artery**. Carbon dioxide in your blood then gets dropped off in the lungs.

Step 3. Oxygen is picked up from the lungs, and the newly oxygenated blood flows to the **left atrium**...

Step 4. ... and into the **left ventricle**.

Step 5. Blood is pumped into the **aorta** and then into the rest of your body.

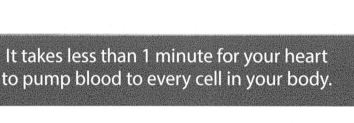

It takes less than 1 minute for your heart to pump blood to every cell in your body.

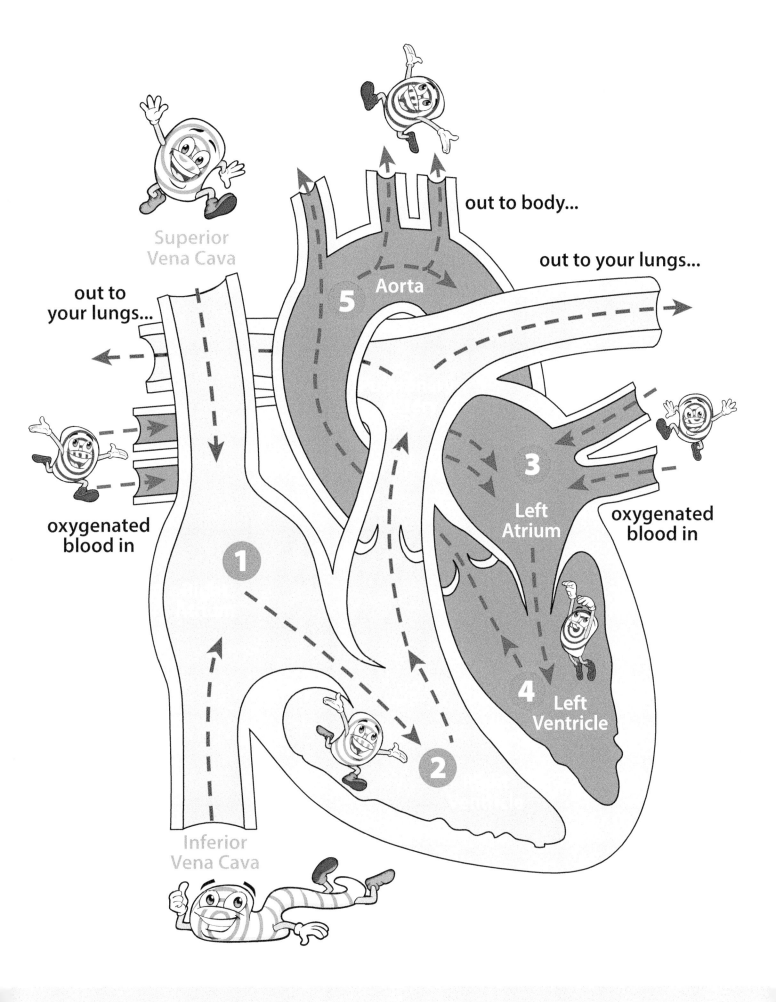

Superior
Vena Cava

out to
your lungs...

out to body...

out to your lungs...

5 Aorta

oxygenated
blood in

oxygenated
blood in

3

Left
Atrium

1

4

Left
Ventricle

2

Inferior
Vena Cava

THE CIRCULATORY SYSTEM

Blood on the Move

Arteries and veins need some help to move substances like oxygen, water, and wastes out of the blood. This is where the capillaries come in. Take a look below to see how all of your blood vessels work together.

Capillaries

are the smallest blood vessels - with walls only one cell thick. The thin walls allow oxygen, nutrients, and wastes to pass between tissues and blood. Almost all of the oxygen leaves the blood here and is used by muscles to make energy.

Arteries

manage the speed and direction of blood. They are large blood vessels carrying oxygenated blood.

Arterioles

regulate the flow of blood to other tissues. They are tiny branches of arteries filled with oxygenated blood.

Venules

drain blood from capillaries into veins, for a return to the heart. They are very small vessels.

Veins

carry deoxygenated blood back to the heart. Their walls are thinner than arteries.

What's the REAL color of your blood?

In drawings, arteries are usually shown as red (for oxygenated blood) and veins are shown as blue (for deoxygenated blood), but all blood has a reddish color.

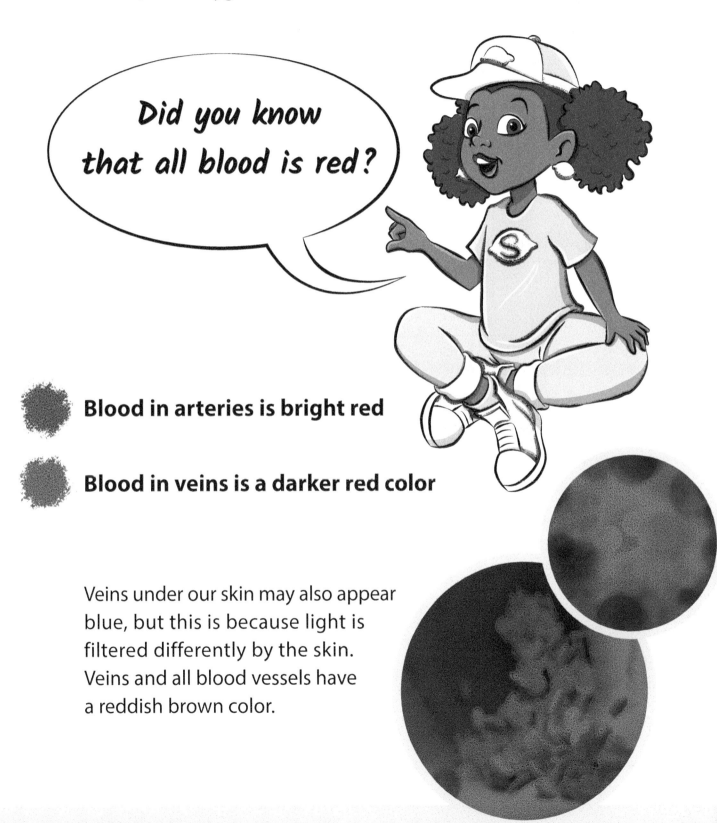

Did you know that all blood is red?

Blood in arteries is bright red

Blood in veins is a darker red color

Veins under our skin may also appear blue, but this is because light is filtered differently by the skin. Veins and all blood vessels have a reddish brown color.

What's In a Drop?

Blood Type

All blood has the same elements (red blood cells, white blood cells, platelets, and plasma), but not all people have the same types of markers on their red blood cells. You can't see blood markers, they are too small to be seen.

Blood markers are also known as antigens. Antigens are the way our bodies identify that our blood belongs to us.

There are 4 major blood groups:

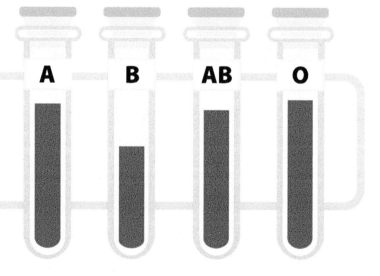

A   B   AB   O

These letters show what types of markers people have on their blood. Doctors use these groups to match patients with blood donors. Some types are considered "universal", meaning they can match with multiple blood types. Type **O negative** is the universal red cell donor. Type **AB** is the universal plasma donor. Like eye color, your blood type is passed genetically from your parents.

Positive or Negative?

You might have heard someone refer to your blood as either negative or positive. That's because some people have another marker, called **Rh factor**, in their blood. Scientists refer to blood as "positive" (meaning it has Rh factor) or "negative" (without Rh factor).

It's important to be sure that donated blood matches the blood type of a person receiving a transfusion.

If someone receives the wrong blood type, this can cause serious health problems.

Rh+ **Rh-**

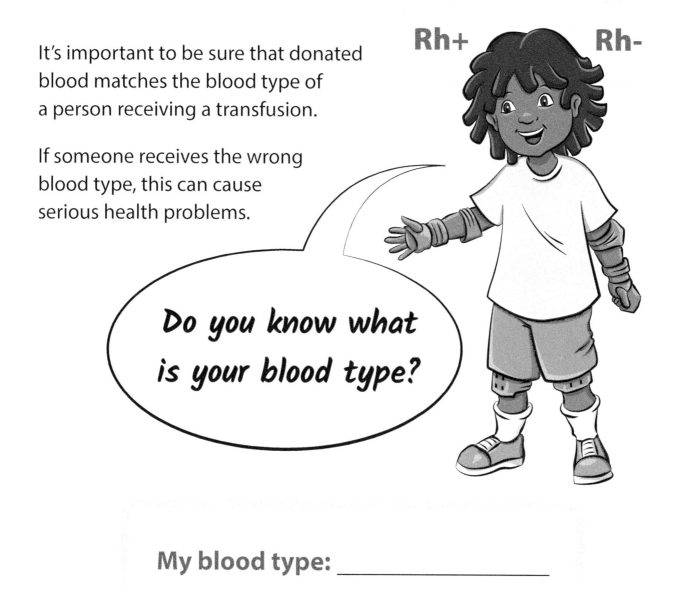

Do you know what is your blood type?

My blood type: _____

Know Your Calm

Stress is mental tension caused by challenges in life, whether they're at school, at home, or anywhere else.

Stress impacts everyone in different ways. It can be as simple as getting annoyed with a friend, hiding your face in a scary movie, or worrying all night about a school quiz.

Everyone's body reacts to stress differently. Some people get headaches, stomach aches, or back pains. It can even make you sleepy and forgetful. No matter how you feel stress, one common result is an increase in your heart rate, or pulse.

This increase happens because your body wants to pump more blood toward your muscles to help you fight dangers or run away from bad situations.

Scientists call this reaction

"fight or flight"

Although it can be helpful in the moment, long-term stress can damage your heart and circulatory system.

Everyone feels stress at times, but how you react to it can have a big impact on your life. Exercising regularly, cultivating a positive attitude, and enjoying a healthy diet are good ways to deal with stress. Sometimes developing and maintaining those valuable habits is tough, especially when you're a kid!

You can also manage your stress through relaxation or meditation techniques.

Check out the **Feel the Beat!** activity (next page), and use it whenever you notice your heart starting to race or you're feeling overwhelmed.

Feel the Beat:
Taking a Trip Through Your Body

Can you feel the blood carrying oxygen through your body? Maybe not. So, let's do an experiment that will show you exactly how it works.

Materials:

- **Stopwatch**

Directions:

1. Stand beside a desk with your stopwatch nearby.

2. On the inside of your wrist on the thumb side, put two fingers over the blood vessel and see if you can feel a tiny beat. That is your pulse!

3. Once you have found your pulse, set your stopwatch for 20 seconds and count how many beats you feel during that time.

4. Then take the number you felt and multiply it by 3.

_____ x 3 = _____

The number you reached is your resting pulse.
This number will likely fall somewhere between 60–100 for a kid your age.
Don't panic if your number is higher or lower.

You may have made a mistake in your calculations, or this activity has made your heart extra excited!

5. Now set your stopwatch for one minute and start running in place — nice and fast. Knees up!

6. When you're done, take your pulse the exact same way as before.

_____ x 3 = _____

The number will be a lot higher now.
Let's examine why.

Are you breathing harder?

That's because your body is asking the heart for more oxygen (or air) to handle all that hard work. In response, your heart is pumping faster to get that oxygen where it needs to go.

Heartbeat Hopscotch

Did you know your heart is a muscle?

The heart is responsible for supporting your movement, as well as helping you breath, eat, and drink. With every heartbeat, the heart is delivering oxygen and nutrients to the body. The blood also transports carbon dioxide* and waste products out of the body.

One heartbeat cycle starts when blood from the body enters the heart from the inferior and superior vena cava*. It flows from the right atrium to the right ventricle, and then to the lungs. In the lungs, blood releases carbon dioxide and waste products and picks up oxygen. Then the blood travels back to the heart's left atrium. From there, it moves from the left atrium to the left ventricle and is pumped out to the body.

This cycle takes place in just one second!

*Say them like this:

carbon dioxide - "CAR-bin die-OX-ide"
vena cava - "VANE-uh KAV-uh"

The strongest syllable is always shown in CAPITALS and red.

Adventurer, how quickly can you complete the heartbeat hopscotch on the next page? One round equals one heartbeat cycle.

Materials:

- **Sidewalk chalk**

Directions:

1. Create a simple Heartbeat Hopscotch by copying the hopscotch of the next page using your sidewalk chalk (ask an adult to help you find the best area for your hopscotch). Make sure each square is at least 1 foot-by-1 foot, but don't worry if your lines aren't perfect!

2. Travel like the flow of blood. Complete a heartbeat cycle by hopping through your hopscotch drawing.

3. Quiz yourself to see if you know your heart beat cycle by describing the cycle with your eyes closed.

Did you know that your heart beats 60 to 100 times a minute? That is over 100,000 times a day!

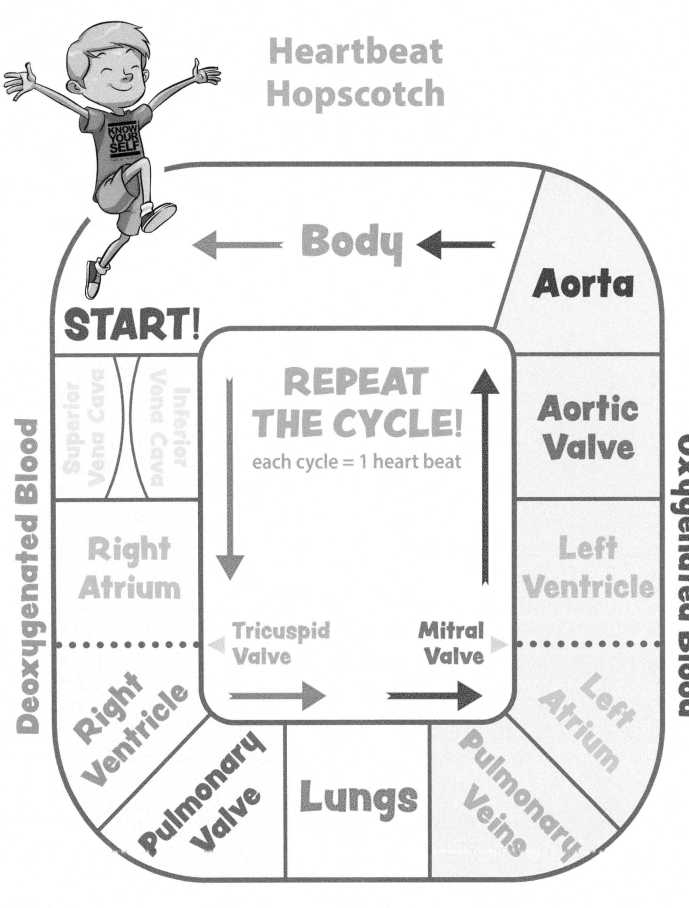

Heartbeat Hopscotch

Heartbeat Hopscotch

If you would like more of a challenge, try drawing a real heart like the one below. Hop through it to get in touch with your inner heart beat.

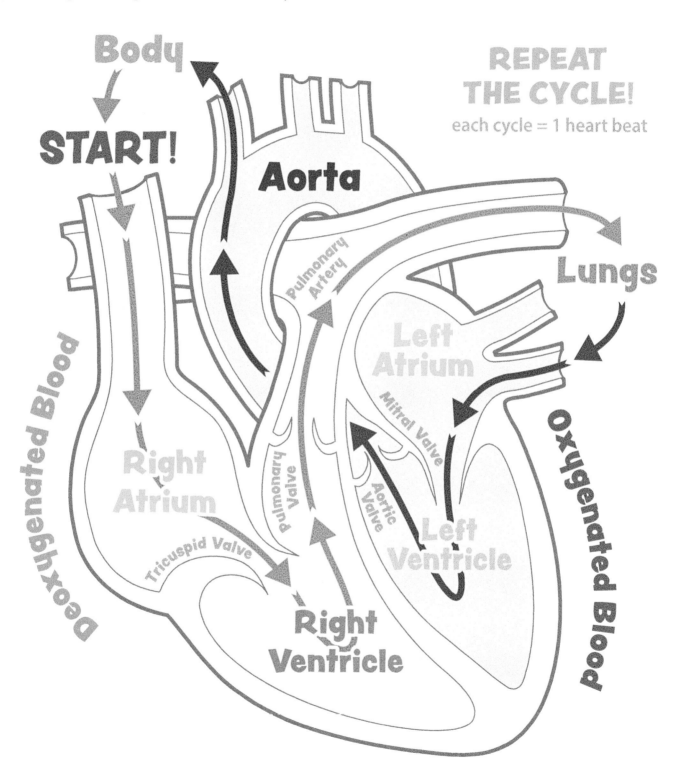

Make a Heart Pump

Use the blue straw to represent an aorta and the red straw to represent a vein in this heart pumping activity. The jar acts like your heart and the extra piece of balloon acts like a valve, making sure that blood pumps from one chamber to another without flowing backwards!

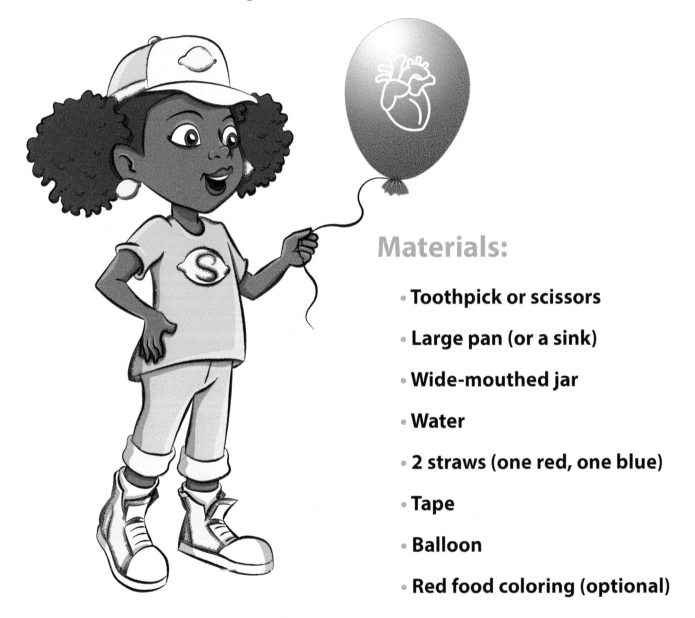

Materials:

- Toothpick or scissors
- Large pan (or a sink)
- Wide-mouthed jar
- Water
- 2 straws (one red, one blue)
- Tape
- Balloon
- Red food coloring (optional)

Directions:

1. Fill your jar halfway with water (add red food coloring to resemble blood).

2. Cut the neck off the balloon and set aside to use in Step 6.

3. Stretch the balloon over the rim of the jar. Pull it down until the balloon fits snugly as a flat surface over the top of the jar.*

4. Using a toothpick (or scissors), make two very small holes in the balloon, approximately one inch apart. The holes should only be large enough to fit the straws through, tightly sealed by the balloon.

5. Push the straws through the holes. If the hole is too large, use tape to seal it.

6. Take the discarded balloon neck from Step 3, fold it in half, and tape it to the end of the blue straw. Make sure that the seal is air-tight.

7. Set the jar in the pan or sink and gently start pressing two fingers on the balloon to start "pumping."

   Now, watch what happens to the water in the jar!

*Grab a friend or parent to help with this step!

Roughly the size of your fist, your heart powers your entire circulatory system.

This single organ has to work against gravity to pump blood up from the legs to the heart, and up from the heart to the head.

Because the heart is so important, we sometimes think of it as not only the center of our bodies, but the center of ourselves.

When we memorize a poem, we say we "**know it by heart**".

A person who is very kind is said to have "**a big heart**" or "**a heart of gold**".

While a person who is sad has a "**broken heart**".

When we encourage someone to do what will make them happy and fulfilled, we tell them to "**follow your heart**".

Even though your actual heart is not where emotions come from, it is vital to staying alive. Just like any muscle, the heart gets stronger when you work it out on a regular basis. Every day you spend time running, skating, climbing – anything that gets your heart pumping – you help this hard-working engine stay tuned up and better able to move nutrient and oxygen-rich blood throughout your body, from head to toe.

Taking care of your heart is necessary for health**!**

As for happiness**?**

Well, we can't say for sure, but in our heart of hearts, we're pretty sure they're related.

Have you ever wondered what your blood flow looks like?

If you have seen it with your own eyes after getting a cut, you may think it looks red and liquidy – but under a microscope it looks much different!

To get a better idea of what it looks like under the lens, try this quick activity.

Materials:

- Clear tupperware or jar

- Water

- Red food coloring

- 1 plastic sealed bag

- O shaped cereal

- White beans

- Lentils

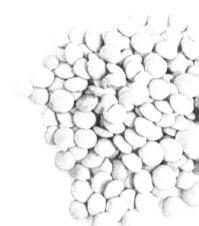

Directions:

1. Take your container and fill it halfway full of water, this water represents the plasma in your bloodstream.

2. Next place your cereal into the plastic bag and add red food coloring. The red cereal serves as your red blood cells.

3. Then pour the red blood cells into the container of water along with a few of the white beans and lentils. The white beans and lentils demonstrate the white blood cells and platelets inside of your blood.

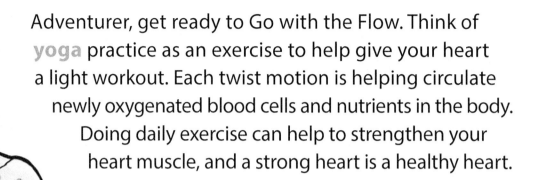

Adventurer, get ready to Go with the Flow. Think of **yoga** practice as an exercise to help give your heart a light workout. Each twist motion is helping circulate newly oxygenated blood cells and nutrients in the body. Doing daily exercise can help to strengthen your heart muscle, and a strong heart is a healthy heart.

When doing yoga, you are actually activating a part of the nervous system called the **parasympathetic*** system. The parasympathetic system is responsible for your body's relaxation response. As you participate in this activity, you will notice the parasympathetic system's effect on your circulatory system. Your breathing, heart rate, and cortisol levels will drop and your blood flow will get a boost in productivity.

The next time you feel a bit stressed, give yourself the gift of yoga. Yoga is all about slowing down. Each pose is held for a few minutes at a time. Connect with your breath and just go with the flow!

***Say it like this:**

parasympathetic - "par-uh-sim-pa-TH-EH-tic"

The strongest syllable is always shown in **CAPITALS** and **red**.

Materials:

- **A soft blanket or a yoga mat**

Directions:

1. Lay out your soft blanket or yoga mat on the floor. This will be your yoga practice area.

2. While on your mat, try to do poses 1 through 10 below and on the next pages. Hold each pose for a minute or two while breathing slowly and deeply.

3. Choose your favorite poses in any order to create your own yoga flow.

3. Grab a friend and see if you can guide them through the yoga flow you created. Have fun!

In the '**Go with the Flow**' activity we learned that yoga could help slow down your heartbeat and make you feel relaxed. Another way to feel calm and gain control over a racing heartbeat is to breathe.

Yes, just breathe!

By taking in deep breaths, fully inhaling and exhaling for a few minutes, we can actually slow down our hearts.

Try it for a few minutes!

Do you feel different afterwards?

coloring opportunity

THE CIRCULATORY SYSTEM

Know Your Circulatory System

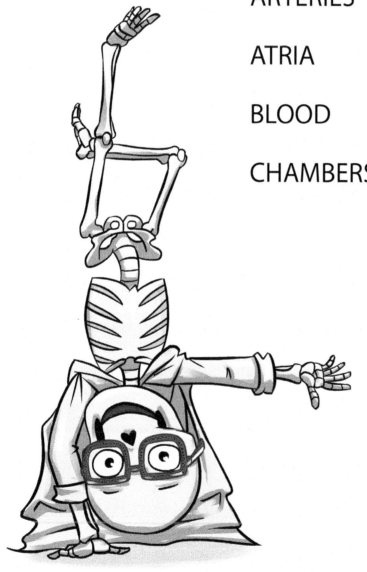

AORTA

ARTERIES

ATRIA

BLOOD

CHAMBERS

CIRCULATORY

HEART

OXYGEN

PULMONARY

VALVES

VEINS

VENACAVA

VENTRICLE

Answer keys on page 112.

```
J U E L O A V P A T M P C Q T W O Z
A T R I A W A C U V I O J M U Y K H
E I M N Q E L Q H L E S S J S V H V
X V O B K X V F V A M N P D O Y B E
C E L W P I E U H E M O T K Q J L I
I Q G S Q H S I Y R N B N R H N O N
C M A O R T A S K I Y A E A I O O S
L C I R C U L A T O R Y C R R C D Z
A R T E R I E S U S L G T A S Y L D
A L I F C F H E A R T R J V V I Q E
C I R X S H K W C G T V O Q T A Q U
T D T O X Y G E N A Y E V M C A F B
```

Good work, adventurers! Now that you know the circulatory system, let's review what you've learned!

Try to fill in the blanks.

The heart plays a central role in your __ __ __ __ __ __ __ __ __ __ __ system.

This strong __ __ __ __ __ __ supports movement, breathing, eating, drinking,

and other daily activities! With the help of your lungs and blood vessels, the

heart moves __ __ __ __ __ throughout your body.

Blood moves through the body to deliver

__ __ __ __ __ __ and nutrients.

Blood also transports __ __ __ __ __ __

__ __ __ __ __ __ and waste

products outside the body.

When your heart beats it counts as one heart ___ ___ ___ ___ ___ . The heart beats

about 60 to 100 times in one ___ ___ ___ ___ ___ ___ !

Daily ___ ___ ___ ___ ___ ___ ___ ___ can help strengthen your heart muscle and ensure

a healthy heart.

Bonus Challenge:

The ___ ___ ___ ___ ___ ___ ___ ___ ___ ___ ___ ___ can impact your

circulatory system by sending out stress or relax signals to the body.

Yoga is one way to ___ ___ ___ ___ ___ when your

heart beat feels higher than normal.

Ready to verify what you have learned?
See the answer key on page 113.

Experience Chinese Foods

China is the fourth-largest country in the world, and food and flavors change from region to region. Many dishes across the country have rice, noodles, vegetables, and meat or tofu to add protein and flavor. A wok, which is a large metal cooking bowl with a round bottom, is one of the most common cooking instruments found throughout China.

Take a look at some of these Chinese-inspired recipes and make something delicious for your family!

Pinky's Hint:

Read through the entire recipe before beginning to prepare food. This way, you'll know what equipment and ingredients are needed, and you'll be familiar with the steps involved.

 Whenever you see the chef's hat icon, it means **you'll need an adult's help**.

*

(Hǎochī)

That means
in Mandarin Chinese.

*Say it like this:

"how-CHIH"

The strongest syllable is always shown in **CAPITALS** and **red**.

Easy Chinese Moon Cakes

In many parts of China, spring and fall are marked by huge festivals. The Chinese calendar is lunar, so the celebration changes with the cycle of the moon. The Spring
Festival celebrates the beginning of the lunar new year, while the Mid-Autumn Festival celebrates the harvest.

It is a time when many Chinese people visit relatives and friends, burn scented incense, and observe the moon, a symbol of harmony and unity. In some parts of China, the festivities include dragon and lion dances, and a variety of delicious moon cakes.

**Prep time:
25 minutes**

**Dough chilling time:
1/2 hour**

**Cooking time:
20 minutes**

Ingredients:

- 2 egg yolks

- 1/2 cup salted butter

- 1/4 cup sugar

- 1 cup all-purpose flour

- 1 cup your favorite jam
  (Traditionally red bean paste is used, so if you want a more authentic version, you can use a can of red bean paste instead of jam)

- Pastry basting brush

 Show off your cooking skills!

Have your grown up take a photo,
and share on social media using the hashtag:

#KnowYourAdventure

 KnowYourselfOAK    KnowYourselfOAK

THE CIRCULATORY SYSTEM

Easy Chinese Moon Cakes

Preparation:

1. Preheat the oven to 375°.

2. In a large bowl, stir 1 egg yolk with the butter and sugar.

3. Mix in the flour to form dough.

4. Form the dough into one large ball and seal it in plastic wrap.

5. Refrigerate dough for 30 minutes.

6. Unwrap the chilled dough and form small balls in the palms of your hand.

7. Make a hole with your thumb in the center of each moon cake and fill it with about 1/2 teaspoon of jam.

8. Beat the second egg yolk.

9. Brush each cake with the beaten egg yolk and place it on a cookie sheet.

10. Bake for about 20 minutes or just until the outside edges are slightly brown.

11. Remove the moon cakes, cool, and enjoy!

Chinese dumplings, also called wontons, are popular all over China. The name wonton means "swallowing clouds". Sounds delicious, right? As the name suggests, these treats have light and fluffy shells, usually filled with minced pork, shrimp, or vegetables.

Making dumplings is a fun team activity for the whole family. One person can add water to the edges of the wrappers, another person can work on filling them, and a third person can seal the ingredients into the wrappers.

**Prep time:
30 to 40 minutes**

**Cooking time:
15 to 20 minutes**

**Makes
50 dumplings**

Chinese Dumplings

Ingredients:

- 5 cups finely shredded Chinese cabbage (approximately 2/3 to 1 whole)
- 1 tablespoon salt
- 1–2 pounds ground meat (pork, turkey, chicken, or beef) or tofu
- 1/2–1 tablespoon minced fresh ginger root
- 1–2 tablespoons thinly sliced green onion
- 3–5 tablespoons soy sauce OR pinch of salt to taste
- 1 tablespoon sesame oil
- 2–4 cloves garlic minced (optional)
- 1 egg beaten (optional)
- 50 round wonton wrappers (store-bought)

Preparation:

1. In a large bowl, mix the shredded cabbage with 1 tablespoon of salt. Set aside for 10–15 minutes.

2. In another large bowl, combine ground meat or tofu, ginger, green onion, soy sauce, sesame oil, gralic, and egg (remember, the garlic and the egg are optional), and mix well.

3. After 10–15 minutes have passed, squeeze out the water from the cabbage.

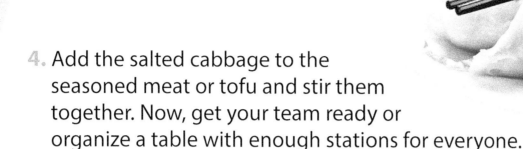

4. Add the salted cabbage to the seasoned meat or tofu and stir them together. Now, get your team ready or organize a table with enough stations for everyone.

5. Place 1 teaspoon of ground meat or tofu filling onto each round wrapper.

6. Moisten the edge with water and fold edge over to form a half-circle shape.

7. Pinch side to seal in filling.

8. Set dumplings aside on a lightly floured surface until ready to cook.

Cooking:

 1. Prepare a large pot with water and bring it to a boil.

 2. Use a large spoon to gently place just enough dumplings in boiling water so they move freely and aren't too crowded in the pot.

3. Stir carefully every 30 seconds, letting the dumplings cook for about 12–15 minutes.

 4. When the pot starts to boil, add more water to keep the level close to the top.

 5. When the dumplings are floating they are ready and you can remove them with the spoon.

6. Serve the dumplings with dipping sauce and enjoy!

What did you learn about Chinese food that you didn't know before this adventure?

_____

_____

_____

Know Yourself Adventure Recipe

Review the recipes from this adventure with what you eat. Record the similarities and differences in the Venn Diagram below.

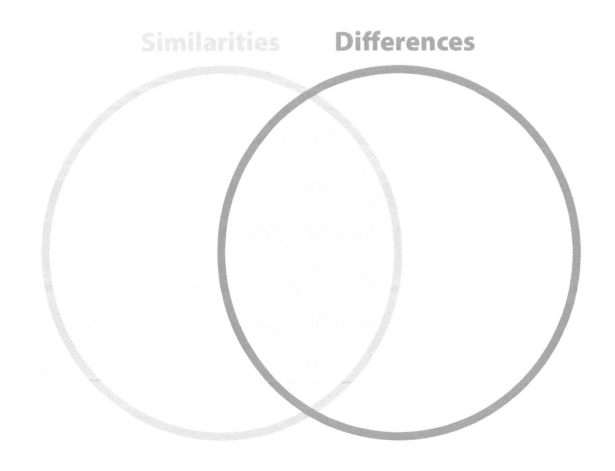

Similarities   Differences

What type of food are you inspired to make next?

_____

_____

_____

_____

_____

_____

_____

 Show off your cooking skills!
Have your grown up take a photo,
and share on social media using the hashtag:

#KnowYourAdventure

 KnowYourselfOAK   KnowYourselfOAK

Cumulative Information Review

Great work, Adventurer!

It's time to get pumped up one more time to show all that you know about Ancient China and your circulatory system. High five a friend when you're all finished with these questions!

Describe a time where you followed your heart.

_____

_____

_____

_____

_____

_____

_____

Describe a time where you felt like your heart was broken. What did you do to feel better?

_____

_____

_____

_____

_____

_____

_____

_____

_____

_____

Cumulative
Information Review

Kung Fu is based on movement and breathing exercises. By learning about how their own bodies work, the monks found it possible to gain more control over themselves, which allowed them to do things others might have found impossible.

Now that you've learned about the heart and how your circulatory system works, how can you use that knowledge in your own life to give yourself more control over your own body and mind?

_____

_____

_____

_____

_____

_____

_____

_____

Describe what it would be like to journey from Ancient China on the Silk Road.

_____

_____

_____

_____

_____

_____

_____

_____

_____

_____

History Resources

Nonfiction

The Heart: Our Circulatory System
Simon, Seymour; Ages 7-10

Fiction

Ancient China: An Interactive History Adventure
(You Choose: Historical Eras)
Collins, Terry; Ages 7-12

History

- *History for Kids*

  This fun, colorful site contains a large amount of varied information suitable for younger readers or for those looking for basic information on a wide variety of topics.

  https://www.historyforkids.net/ancient-china.html

- *Britannica Kids*

  For students looking for more information that is adaptable to their reading or interest level, Britannica Kids offers three levels of detail and information covering all aspects of China, from its history to the plants and animals found there.

  https://kids.britannica.com/students/article/China/272682#195666-toc

NEXT
The Renal System

4

Get a good night's sleep before this adventure
because when you fall into **Ancient Assyria in Northern Iraq**. . . you will
need to be on your toes. **The year is 810 BCE** and the renal system is under
inspection in . . . **YOU'VE GOT TO BE KIDNEY!**

THE CIRCULATORY SYSTEM

THE CIRCULATORY SYSTEM

TO BE CONTINUED...

THE CIRCULATORY SYSTEM

How to Draw Dr. Bonyfide!

Today I'm going to teach you how to draw Dr. Bonyfide!

Start with a simple oval for Dr. B's head. Then draw horizontal and vertical lines through the center. This will help you place his facial features.

Next draw simple circles on the horizontal lines and a triangle in the middle of the vertical line. These will be his eyes and nose. Also, add in a smile for his mouth!

Dr. B doesn't see very well, so add in squares for his glasses. And don't forget his eyebrows!

Now that you have everything positioned, start detailing them. This is where your drawing will really start to take shape.

Erase out your sketch lines (or you can go over your drawing in ink as well) and *voila!*

Dr. B never looked so good!

Now try it yourself!

 Share your drawing on social media so I can see it:

#KnowYourAdventure

 KnowYourselfOAK   KnowYourselfOAK

THE CIRCULATORY SYSTEM

Ancient China Crossword

Know Your History
Information Review

Shaolin monks did not always practice Kung Fu; this practice was introduced by

Da Mo , a monk from India . In the year 527, he visited a Shaolin

Temple to spread the teachings of Buddhism .

Kung Fu means learned skill and was originally a series

of movements and breathing .

The blocks and strikes that evolved and which the martial art is known for were

named after the animals that inspired them.

Tianyuan was a famous Chinese monk asked to help defend the

country from pirates . Using an iron bar, he defeated eight

monks with swords to earn the right to lead.

Despite its martial utility, Kung Fu was primarily studied to aid the monks in their

quest to know themselves .

Answer Keys

Circulatory System Word Search

```
J U E L O A V P A T M P C Q T W O Z
A T R I A W A C U V I O J M U Y K H
E I M N Q E L Q H L E S S J S V H V
X V O B K X V F V A M N P D O Y B E
C E L W P I E U H E M O T K Q J L I
I Q G S Q H S I Y R N B N R H N O N
C M A O R T A S K I Y A E A I O O S
L C I R C U L A T O R Y C R R C D Z
A R T E R I E S U S L G T A S Y L D
A L I F C F H E A R T R J V V I Q E
C I R X S H K W C G T V O Q T A Q U
T D T O X Y G E N A Y E V M C A F B
```

Know Your Circulatory System
Information Review

The heart plays a central role in your c i r c u l a t o r y system.

This strong m u s c l e supports movement, breathing, eating, drinking,

and other daily activities! With the help of your lungs and blood vessels, the

heart moves b l o o d throughout your body.

Blood moves through the body to deliver o x y g e n and nutrients.

Blood also transports c a r b o n   d i o x i d e and waste

products outside the body.

When your heart beats it counts as one heart c y c l e . The heart beats

about 60 to 100 times in one m i n u t e !

Daily e x e r c i s e can help strengthen your heart muscle and ensure

a healthy heart.

Bonus Challenge:

The n e r v o u s   s y s t e m can impact your

circulatory system by sending out stress or relax signals to the body.

Yoga is one way to r e l a x when your heart beat

feels higher than normal.

CREATED WITH LOVE
BY THE
KNOW YOURSELF TEAM